W9-DHV-728

1 9 8 5
The Year You Were Born

Birth Certificate

Name: _____

Birthdate: _____

Time: _____

Place of Birth: _____

Weight: _____ Length: _____

Mother's maiden name: _____

Father's name: _____

To Christopher and Scott Graham from Auntie Jeanne   J.M.

To Auntie Helen, with love   J.L.

Text copyright © 1992 by Jeanne Martinet
Illustrations copyright © 1992 by Judy Lanfredi
All rights reserved. No part of this book may be reproduced
or utilized in any form or by any
means, electronic or
mechanical, including photocopying, recording, or by any
information storage or retrieval system, without permission in
writing from the Publisher. Inquiries should be addressed to
Tambourine Books, a division of William Morrow & Company, Inc.,
1350 Avenue of the Americas, New York, New York 10019.
Printed in the U.S.A.

Library of Congress Cataloging in Publication Data
Martinet, Jeanne (Jeanne M.)
The year you were born, 1985/compiled by Jeanne Martinet;
illustrated by Judy Lanfredi. — 1st ed.
p. cm.
Summary: Presents an assortment of events, news items,
and facts for each day of the year 1985.
ISBN 0-688-11081-9 (trade). — ISBN 0-688-11082-7 (lib.)
1. Nineteen eighty-five, A.D.—Chronology—Juvenile literature.
2. United States—History—1969- —Chronology—Juvenile literature.
[1. Calendars. 2. Nineteen eighty-five, A.D.—Chronology.]
I. Lanfredi, Judy, ill. II. Title.
E876.M365 1992 031.02—dc20 91-37439 CIP AC

1 3 5 7 9 10 8 6 4 2
First edition

1 9 8 5
The Year You Were Born

Compiled by

JEANNE MARTINET

Illustrated by

JUDY LANFREDI

Tambourine Books • New York

U.S. Almanac
1985

International Youth Year

Halley's Comet Year

United States population
239,283,000
Males 116,649,000
Females 122,634,000

Size of U.S.
3,618,770 square miles

President
Ronald Reagan

Largest city
New York, population 7,164,742

Biggest state (in area)
Alaska, 591,004 square miles

Number of births in U.S.
3,761,000
Boys 1,928,000
Girls 1,833,000
Average length at birth 1 foot 8 inches
Average weight at birth 7½ pounds

Deaths in U.S.
2,086,000

Number of children ages 5 to 13
30,110,000
Tornadoes 684

Households with television sets
84,900,000

Households with VCRs
20.8 percent of all homes

Top crop
Corn

Total 1985 output
225 million metric tons

Beverages consumed
140.3 gallons per person
(including 45.6 gallons of soft drinks and 27.1 gallons of milk)

Automobiles (and light trucks) purchased
15,600,000

Children's books sold
210,000,000

Top movie (highest earnings)
Back to the Future, $190 million

Top spectator sport
Baseball, which drew 47,742,000 fans

Top dog
Cocker spaniel—96,396 American Kennel Club registrations

Boy Scouts 3,755,000
Girl Scouts 2,172,000

Most popular girl's name Jessica

Most popular boy's name Michael

Most rain
Mobile, Alabama, 69.97 inches

Most snow
Marquette, Michigan, 269.3 inches

January

January is named after Janus, the Roman god of doorways and of beginnings.

BIRTHSTONE *Garnet*

TUESDAY
January 1

New Year's Day • A fierce midwestern blizzard knocks out electric power to 260,000 homes and businesses in Illinois and Michigan.

WEDNESDAY
January 2

Prime Minister Yasuhiro Nakasone of Japan meets with President Ronald Reagan in Los Angeles.

THURSDAY
January 3

The 99th session of the United States Congress opens in Washington, D.C. • In Fort Worth, Texas, 720 pounds of chili is stolen from a restaurant.

FRIDAY
January 4

Dr. William Grant of Iowa performed the first appendectomy in history 100 years ago today. • The U.S. grants political asylum to Soviet atomic physicist Vladimirovich Kulikov.

SATURDAY
January 5

RARE-BIRD ALERT: The Bobolinks, a national network of bird-watchers, have issued a rare-bird alert. The Eurasian bean goose has been spotted near Blair, Nebraska.

SUNDAY
January 6

Alaska celebrates its purchase of the 530-mile-long Alaska Railroad from the U.S. government with a ceremony that features a gold switch key—and buffalo stew!

MONDAY
January 7

Full Moon

Kazoo expert Barbara Stewart, author of *How to Kazoo*, gives kazoo lessons to the passengers on board a plane going from Newark, New Jersey, to London, England.

TUESDAY
January 8

To celebrate the late singer's 50th birthday, Elvis Presley fan clubs give 170 teddy bears to a children's center in Memphis, Tennessee. • Jackie A. Strange becomes the first woman in U.S. history to be named deputy postmaster general.

WHO ELSE WAS BORN IN JANUARY?
ALICE PAUL

Feminist, lawyer, leader of the woman suffrage movement and then the first campaign for an equal rights amendment in the early 1900s.
She became the national chairperson of the National Woman's Party in 1942.
BORN January 11, 1885, in Moorestown, New Jersey

WEDNESDAY
January 9

Scientists from 30 countries discuss the future of Antarctica at an international conference held on the Ross Ice Shelf, 450 miles from the South Pole.

THURSDAY
January 10

America's first children's space program, the Young Astronaut Program, begins at Viking Elementary School in Grand Forks, North Dakota.

FRIDAY
January 11

The Greek government bars overweight people from driving. Driver's licenses will no longer be issued to anyone more than 70 percent heavier than normal.

SATURDAY
January 12

The U.S. Fish and Wildlife Service reports that the wood stork and the woodland caribou have been added to the list of endangered species.

SUNDAY
January 13

Record-breaking snowstorm (13 inches) hits San Antonio, Texas. • Ornithologists at Poyang Lake Bird Sanctuary in China count a total of 1,350 great white cranes—the largest flock of cranes in the world.

MONDAY
January 14

Adam Azzam from Damascus, Syria, has reached Washington, D.C., after completing a 3,800-mile leg of his trip around the world on horseback. So far, he has stayed in 700 homes along the way.

FUN FACT '85

Airtime for a 30-second commercial during the 1985 Super Bowl costs $525,000.

TUESDAY
January 15

Anniversary of the birth of Martin Luther King, Jr. • The U.S. Supreme Court rules that public school officials may search students who are suspected of breaking a law or a school rule.

WEDNESDAY
January 16

South Dakota gets 18 inches of snow. The bitter cold "Arctic express" air from Canada is headed for the East Coast!

THURSDAY
January 17

Kathleen Castro, age 11, of Loggers Run Middle School in Boca Raton, Florida, has been chosen the winner of the *Weekly Reader* elementary school "Goals for Our President" national essay contest. Her entry was about world peace.

FRIDAY
January 18

Daniel Webster was born on this day in 1782; A. A. Milne in 1882; Cary Grant in 1904; and Muhammad Ali in 1942.

HAPPY BIRTHDAY

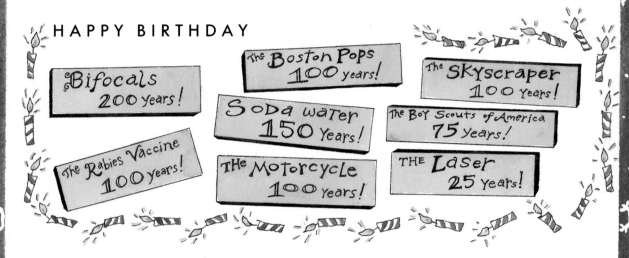

Bifocals 200 years!

The Boston Pops 100 years!

The Skyscraper 100 years!

Soda water 150 years!

The Boy Scouts of America 75 years!

The Rabies Vaccine 100 years!

The Motorcycle 100 years!

The Laser 25 years!

SATURDAY
January 19

A 900-pound, 13-foot-long, 21-year-old alligator named Ole Hardhide is buried in Ponchatoula, Louisiana. The funeral features a horse-drawn casket, a jazz band, and a speech by the mayor.

SUNDAY
January 20

SUPER BOWL XIX: Football's San Francisco 49ers triumph over the Miami Dolphins, 38-16, in Palo Alto, California. • Chicago, Illinois, hits a record low temperature of 27 degrees below zero.

MONDAY
January 21

Inauguration Day, and the coldest day on record in more than 80 U.S. cities! President Ronald Reagan is publicly sworn in for a second term. The inaugural parade is canceled due to the freezing weather.

TUESDAY
January 22

The government of Thailand asks its people to release 9,999,999 fish from captivity to help Queen Sirikit recover from an operation. The symbolic freeing of the fish is supposed to bring good luck.

WEDNESDAY
January 23

The space shuttle *Discovery* liftoff is postponed because of ice on the launching tower at the Kennedy Space Center in Cape Canaveral, Florida.

THE FRAGGLES ARE BACK

The happy-go-lucky Muppets, created by Jim Henson, begin their third year on the television show *Fraggle Rock*. The Fraggles are Mokey, Boober, Gobo, Red, Wembley, the Gorgs, and the Doozers!

THURSDAY
January 24

In Portland, Oregon, Penny E. Harrington becomes the first woman to head the police force of a major city. • *Discovery* is launched from Cape Canaveral, Florida, on a top-secret military mission.

FRIDAY
January 25

James Sciuto of Methuen, Massachusetts, has created a gigantic ice sculpture in his backyard, using chicken wire, a garden hose, 250,000 gallons of water, and a week of below-freezing temperatures!

SATURDAY
January 26

Michigan receives the first of 30 moose from Ontario, Canada, which the state is getting in exchange for 150 wild turkeys. • Lawrence University in Appleton, Wisconsin, holds its 20th annual Midwest Trivia Contest.

SUNDAY
January 27

Space shuttle *Discovery* lands with a perfect touchdown in Cape Canaveral, Florida. • Lori Hendricks of Indianapolis, Indiana, wins the Barbie doll look-alike contest. She won a Joan Rivers look-alike contest last year!

MONDAY
January 28

In Buffalo, New York, 4 feet of snow left by an 8-day blizzard caused the roof of a department store to collapse.

TUESDAY
January 29

Workers at the Smithsonian Institution's Air and Space Museum begin removing the famous Wright brothers' 1903 Flyer, the first power-driven airplane ever flown. They are taking it down to be restored.

WEDNESDAY
January 30

Soviet newspapers report a Russian sighting of a UFO (unidentified flying object). The crew and passengers on board an airplane flying over Minsk saw "a large, unblinking star" which shot out beams of light and then left a green cloud in its wake.

THURSDAY
January 31

2,000 Florida mosquitoes are put on a plane to Minneapolis, Minnesota, where they will become food for carnivorous plants at the Home and Garden Show.

INAUGURATION TRIVIA

- Thomas Jefferson was the first President to be inaugurated in Washington, D.C.—in 1801.
- The longest speech at an inauguration was given by William Henry Harrison in 1841, in extremely cold weather. It lasted 90 minutes.
- The coldest inauguration day in history was that of Ulysses S. Grant in 1873. It was 16°F.
- The most expensive inaugural celebration was held in 1981 for Ronald Reagan. It cost $15,500,000!

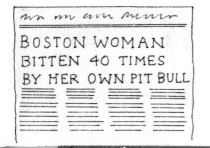

BOSTON WOMAN BITTEN 40 TIMES BY HER OWN PIT BULL

ANGRY ROCKETTES PICKET RADIO CITY MUSIC HALL

WORST COLD WAVE OF THE CENTURY OVER MUCH OF U.S.

February

*T*he name February comes from the Latin *Februa*, which means "feast of purification."

BIRTHSTONE *Amethyst*

FRIDAY
February 1

Greenland withdraws from the European Economic Community. • Three earth tremors registering 5.6 on the Richter scale are felt in Iran. • Fires caused by lack of rain have been burning in south Florida for a month.

SATURDAY
February 2

Groundhog Day • In Kansas City, Missouri, the U.S. figure-skating championships are won by Tiffany Chin in women's singles and by Brian Boitano in men's singles.

SUNDAY
February 3

National New Idea Week • Today is winter's halfway point. It's boiling hot in Florida and freezing cold in the rest of the country!

MONDAY
February 4

In Naples, Italy, 251 suspected gangsters go on trial. • There's a bean-throwing festival in Japan.

TUESDAY
February 5
Full Moon

The 1985 Albert Schweitzer International Prize for Medicine is given to Dr. Donald A. Henderson for helping to rid the world of smallpox.

WEDNESDAY
February 6

President Reagan's staff presents a cake to him in the Oval Office of the White House for his 74th birthday.

THURSDAY
February 7

The Soviet icebreaker *Moskva* begins a rescue operation to try to free more than 1,000 white whales that are trapped in the ice off northeast Siberia. • The first video cattle auction takes place in Omaha, Nebraska. The 7,015 cows are home at their ranches while videos of them are shown to the bidders.

FRIDAY
February 8

Today is the 75th anniversary of the Boy Scouts of America; the nation's top scouts lunch with President Reagan. • Basketball player Bruce Morris of Marshall University in Huntington, West Virginia, breaks the record for a long shot when he makes a basket from 89 feet 10 inches down the court.

WHO ELSE WAS BORN IN FEBRUARY?
CHARLES DARWIN

British naturalist
He became famous for his development of the theory of evolution and for his book *Origin of Species*.
BORN February 12, 1809, in Shrewsbury, England

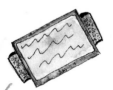

SATURDAY
February 9

A crew that has been trying to remove a Venezuelan ship that ran aground beside a millionaire's swimming pool in Palm Beach, Florida, last Thanksgiving drags the ship 10 feet today. Millionaire Mollie Wilmot has her first clear view of the ocean since November!

SUNDAY
February 10

At the 18th annual National Inventors Exposition in Arlington, Virginia, more than 50 inventors demonstrate their new inventions. In addition, 6 people are inducted into the National Inventors Hall of Fame, including the inventors of air conditioning, Willis Haviland Carrier; tape recording, Marvin Camras; and Teflon, Roy J. Plunkett.

SOME INVENTIONS OF 1985

February 11 is National Inventors Day

The flat-screen television set
Cabbage Patch doll braces (for teeth!)
The bionic house
Turbine skis
The electric bandage
The one-handed spice mill

The crayfish harvester
Personal I.D.'s on teeth
The homemade tornado
Cellular pay phones
The flag-waving machine

The first National Invention Contest for Children is held in 1985, sponsored by *Weekly Reader*, the National Council of Patent Law Associations, and the U.S. Patent and Trademark Office. 80,000 kids of all ages enter. Among the winners:

Suzie Amling, for her "Line leader and keeper"
Katie Harding, for her "Mud puddle spotter"
Ryan Johnson, for his "Keep-warm bird feeder"
Kim Mehuron, for his "Jim-dandy unlosable toothpaste cap"

Mark Mueller, for his "Cereal plate"
Clint Vaught, for his "Logg Hogg lifting arm"
James R. Wollin, for his "Jar of plenty"

MONDAY
February 11

STORMS GALORE! Snow and rain cover the North-west and Midwest, and there are thunderstorms and tornadoes in the South. • The American International Toy Fair opens in New York City.

TUESDAY
February 12

Lincoln's Birthday • At the Westminster Kennel Club dog show, a female Scottish terrier, Ch. Braeburn's Close Encounter (better known as Shannon), wins best-in-show. Shannon has won a record 186 best-in-show prizes.

WEDNESDAY
February 13

During a training mission, a marine pilot is forced to crash-land his fighter jet in the space between 2 houses in Pensacola, Florida. He parachutes out at the last minute!

THURSDAY
February 14

Valentine's Day. Americans exchange an estimated 900,000,000 greeting cards. • Snowdrifts of up to 12 feet bring parts of the Midwest to a standstill; in Ohio and Indiana, the mail carriers can't even get through! The mayor of Richmond, Kentucky, postpones Valentine's Day because of a snowstorm.

FRIDAY
February 15

Officials in Moscow call a halt to the world championship chess match between Anatoly Karpov and Gary Kasparov after 6 months of playing a record 48 games. The players are too exhausted to continue.

SATURDAY
February 16

The United Nations famine relief operation sends 19 ships with 130,000 tons of food to Ethiopia. • A 6-foot-tall stuffed gorilla is auctioned off for $20,350 in New York City.

SUNDAY
February 17

Richard Binzel, an astronomer at McDonald Observatory in Texas, becomes the first person to see the eclipse of the planet Pluto by its moon. Pluto is 2,800,000,000 miles from Earth.

MONDAY
February 18

On board a commuter plane 4,000 feet over Alaska, 2 strapped-in passengers hold on to a copilot's legs while he lies on his belly to close a door that opened accidentally 5 minutes after takeoff.

TUESDAY *February 19*	**MICKEY MOUSE VISITS CHINA:** Mickey is welcomed with a tour of the Great Wall of China and a Peking duck dinner. His visit is part of a worldwide tour to mark Disneyland's 30th anniversary.
WEDNESDAY *February 20*	Beginning of the Chinese Year of the Ox • Prime Minister Margaret Thatcher of Great Britain addresses the U.S. Congress in Washington, D.C. She is the first British Prime Minister to address congress since Winston Churchill in 1952.
THURSDAY *February 21*	Spring is coming! Mexican gold poppies are beginning to open in Organ-Pipe Cactus National Monument in Arizona. • Fires destroy 2,500 acres of land near Naples, Florida.

1985: CHINESE YEAR OF THE OX
February 20, 1985–February 8, 1986

According to legend, Buddha summoned all the animals in the world—promising them a reward. Only 12 obeyed, and he gave them each a year. The Rat arrived first, so he got the first year. The order of the 12-year cycle is always the same: Rat, Ox, Tiger, Hare, Dragon, Snake, Horse, Sheep, Monkey, Rooster, Dog, and Pig.

Oxen are quiet and patient. They are often very intelligent and can make good leaders. They work hard and are good with their hands, but they can be a bit stubborn! Oxen tend to be very fond of their families. They get along well with Roosters and Rats but not with Monkeys, Sheep, or Tigers. Famous Oxen include Aristotle, Napoleon, Vincent Van Gogh, Charlie Chaplin, Walt Disney, Henry David Thoreau, King Richard the Lion-Heart, King Louis XIII, Gerald Ford, Hans Christian Andersen, Warren Harding, David Carradine, Dustin Hoffman, Jack Nicholson, Billy Joel, B. B. King, and Bill Cosby.

FRIDAY
February 22

George Washington's birthday • The town of Alton, Illinois, celebrates the 67th anniversary of the birth of Robert Pershing Wadlow, the tallest man in history at 8 feet 11 inches, with an exhibit and flowers.

SATURDAY
February 23

Toilets are frozen at the Lincolnville, Maine, ferry terminal. Officials say they won't thaw until mid-April.

FUN FACT '85

Mickey Mouse's name in Chinese is Xishu.

西鼠

SUNDAY
February 24

Seventy-five fires are burning in grasslands and forests across Florida. Since the beginning of the year, there have been 3,021 brushfires in the state.

MONDAY
February 25

Melting snow causes flooding in Indiana, Illinois, Oklahoma, Mississippi, Pennsylvania, and New York. • A 10-year-old gets a $2,000 reward in Raleigh, North Carolina, for identifying the killers of a rare sea turtle.

TUESDAY
February 26

In Hyattsville, Maryland, maintenance worker Bob Alcombright stops on his way to work to catch a man leaping out of a burning house.

WEDNESDAY
February 27

A pretzel company that provides 50,000 soft pretzels daily to the Philadelphia, Pennsylvania, area starts up again after being shut down for 2 days because of a broken conveyor belt. Philadelphia's pretzel lovers rejoice!

THURSDAY
February 28

In Mississippi, 60,000 students get a temporary holiday from school because 2,500 teachers are on strike. • The launch of the space shuttle *Challenger* is delayed for the third time.

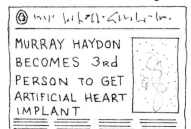

MURRAY HAYDON BECOMES 3rd PERSON TO GET ARTIFICIAL HEART IMPLANT

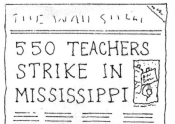

THE WALL STREET

550 TEACHERS STRIKE IN MISSISSIPPI

TOWN IN KENTUCKY POSTPONES VALENTINE'S DAY

March

March is named for the Roman god of war, Mars.
BIRTHSTONE *Aquamarine*

FRIDAY
March 1

The U.S. Bureau of the Census reports that Americans would rather walk than go fishing, jog, or play tennis or golf.

SATURDAY
March 2

A Dr. Seuss birthday parade is held in Hibbing, Minnesota. • Bird experts are trying to hunt down a mysterious, deadly bird disease which has been reported in 26 states across the U.S.

SUNDAY
March 3

An earthquake shakes Chile. • In the Santa Anita Handicap horse race in Arcadia, California, Willie Shoemaker becomes the first jockey to win $100,000,000 in career purse money.

MONDAY
March 4

Denver, Colorado, holds its first public buffalo auction!

TUESDAY
March 5

A massive rock slide piles debris on a highway near Waynesville, North Carolina.

WEDNESDAY
March 6

National Procrastination Week • The *Mercedes I*, the 197-foot Venezuelan freighter that has been beached in Florida for 10 weeks, is freed today, with the help of high tide!

THURSDAY
March 7
Full Moon

The Soviet Union's Aleksandr Fadeev wins the men's singles competition in the world figure-skating championships in Tokyo, Japan. • Mons Meg, a huge medieval cannon from Scotland, goes on display at the Tower of London in England.

FRIDAY
March 8

International Women's Day • Fifty top recording artists, who have combined their talents for a worthy cause, release the single "We Are the World" to raise money for starving people in Africa.

SATURDAY
March 9

East Germany's Katarina Witt wins her second straight world championship figure-skating title in Tokyo, Japan.

SUNDAY
March 10

Mount Etna in Sicily erupts. A stream of lava more than 2,950 feet long pours from the southeast crater of the volcano.

WHO ELSE WAS BORN IN MARCH?
DR. SEUSS

Children's author and illustrator
Author of more than 50 children's books, he is best known for *The Cat in the Hat* and *Why the Grinch Stole Christmas*. His real name was Theodor Seuss Geisel.
BORN March 2, 1904, in Springfield, Massachusetts

MONDAY
March 11

Johnny Appleseed Day • Mikhail Gorbachev is named the new general secretary of the Soviet Communist Party, making him the new leader of the Soviet Union.

TUESDAY
March 12

Arms-control talks between the Soviet Union and the United States begin in Geneva, Switzerland. • High winds in the Midwestern U.S. knock out electricity to 60,000 homes and businesses.

WEDNESDAY
March 13

A strong earthquake hits western Oregon shortly before noon. • The Coca-Cola Company has agreed to let a man in Guilford, Vermont, who changed his name to Mr. Coke-Is-It, keep his new name—as long as he doesn't use it to make money.

THURSDAY
March 14

The 14th Street Bridge in Washington, D.C., hit by an airliner in 1982, is renamed the Arland D. Williams Memorial Bridge, in honor of the man who gave his life to save victims of the crash.

FRIDAY
March 15

The Ides of March • It is also Buzzard Day in Hinkley, Ohio, the day the town's buzzards return for the summer. • In Newhall, California, Jim Mitchell has grown a 34-inch-wide mustache.

SATURDAY
March 16

Three robbers make off with $5,000,000 in cash and jewelry from an antique gallery in Deerfield Beach, Florida.

SUNDAY
March 17

St. Patrick's Day • First tornado of the season whips through Venice, Florida. • President Reagan and Prime Minister Brian Mulroney of Canada announce that they will set up a joint team of experts to examine the issue of acid rain.

MONDAY
March 18

SPACE HISTORY: Twenty years ago today, cosmonaut Aleksei A. Leonov took the first walk in space.

TUESDAY
March 19

Astrophysicists report that a cosmic power far out in space may be bombarding the earth with subatomic particles different from any currently known to science.

WEDNESDAY
March 20

Spring equinox • After nearly 18 days of traveling through a blinding snowstorm, Libby Riddles becomes the first woman to win the world's longest sled-dog race, the Iditarod Trail International Race from Anchorage to Nome in Alaska. She gives each of her 13 huskies a box of biscuits.

THURSDAY
March 21

At the Audubon Zoo in New Orleans, Louisiana, a cage door is found open and a rare toucan is missing.

FRIDAY
March 22

National Goof-Off Day • NASA's most powerful unmanned rocket, the Atlas Centaur, blasts off from Cape Canaveral in Florida, carrying a $41,000,000 communications satellite.

SATURDAY
March 23

Third annual Cherry Blossom Festival in Macon, Georgia. Macon has 50,000 Yoshino cherry trees, making it America's Cherry Blossom Capital.

SUNDAY
March 24

People from Tennessee to Florida see a strange red, green, and orange fireball streak across the night sky. • In Portugal, Zola Budd of Great Britain wins the first women's world cross-country championship in 15 minutes, 0.1 seconds—running barefoot!

TOP TEN SINGLES OF 1985*

1. "I Want to Know What Love Is" — Foreigner
2. "Careless Whisper" — Wham! featuring George Michael
3. "Can't Fight the Feeling" — REO Speedwagon
4. "One More Night" — Phil Collins
5. "We Are the World" — USA for Africa
6. "Crazy for You" — Madonna
7. "Don't You (Forget About Me)" — Simple Minds
8. "Everything She Wants" — Wham!
9. "Everybody Wants to Rule the World" — Tears For Fears
10. "Heaven" — Bryan Adams

*Source: *Billboard*.

MONDAY
March 25

A "letter of peace" more than 2,000-feet-long is delivered to the U.S. arms-control delegation in Geneva, Switzerland. It is made up of 3,000 letters—taped together end to end—from American schoolchildren who want a peaceful world.

TUESDAY
March 26

NASA officials announce that rats and squirrel monkeys will be blasting off with the seven human astronauts on the next voyage of the space shuttle *Challenger*.

WEDNESDAY
March 27

Publisher Malcolm Forbes buys a rare photograph of Abraham Lincoln with his son Todd for a world-record price of $104,500.

THURSDAY
March 28

Milton, Florida, holds its Scratch Ankle Festival, featuring a parade, a 10,000-meter run, and the Little Mr. and Miss Scratch Ankle pageant. • Measles outbreak in Puerto Rico!

FRIDAY
March 29

The town of Riverside, Iowa, has declared itself to be the birthplace of Captain James T. Kirk, the fictional hero of the TV show *Star Trek*. Riverside's new logo: "Where the Trek Begins."

FUN FACT '85

Rats can go without water longer than camels can.

SATURDAY
March 30

The Venezuelan ship that ran aground last Thanksgiving in Palm Beach, Florida, is blown up and sunk today off the coast of Fort Lauderdale. It will serve as an artificial reef to attract fish.

SUNDAY
March 31

DOG'S BEST FRIEND: A stray German shepherd is found guarding an injured Doberman pinscher on a busy street in Los Angeles. When cars approach, the stray covers the hurt dog's body with its own. • Old Dominion University defeats the University of Georgia in the NCAA women's basketball tournament.

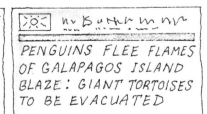

SOVIET LEADER KONSTANTIN CHERNENKO DIES: MIKHAIL GORBACHEV NAMED NEW HEAD

PENGUINS FLEE FLAMES OF GALAPAGOS ISLAND BLAZE: GIANT TORTOISES TO BE EVACUATED

DOG FRISBEE CHAMPION DIES

April

The name April comes from the Latin *aperire*, which means "to open." April is known as the time of budding.

BIRTHSTONE *Diamond*

MONDAY
April 1

HOTEL ON WHEELS: In San Antonio, Texas, the Fairmont Hotel, weighing 3,200,000 pounds, is rolled down the street 4 blocks to a new location. • Villanova University wins the men's NCAA basketball championship. • April Fools' Day.

TUESDAY
April 2

The world's only flock of whooping cranes, currently in Austwell, Texas, is migrating north for the spring. • In Swainsboro, Georgia, Lee Studstill climbs a pine tree, where he plans to stay for 32 days.

WEDNESDAY
April 3

The world's most famous hunter of live dinosaurs, Herman Regusters, is setting out on his second expedition to Africa's Congo jungle to find a strange long-necked, humpbacked, brontosauruslike animal he saw there before.

THURSDAY
April 4

Theresa Knecht Dozier of Columbia, South Carolina, is named Teacher of the Year. She will receive a golden apple from President Reagan at a special White House ceremony.

FRIDAY
April 5
Full Moon

After years of pressure from the U.S. and other countries, Japan agrees to end all commercial whaling (the killing of whales to make products) by 1988.

SATURDAY
April 6

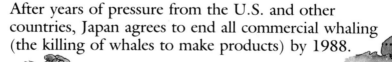

First day of Passover • Paul Butski wins the $5,000 top prize in the All-American Turkey-calling Championship in Scranton, Pennsylvania.

SUNDAY
April 7

Easter • Children scramble for 72,000 hard-boiled and 40,000 candy eggs at the 26th annual Garrison Egg Hunt in Homer, Georgia. In Miami, Florida, marine science students dive for eggs in an underwater egg hunt along Emerald Reef.

MONDAY
April 8

Ronald and Nancy Reagan hold the traditional Easter egg hunt on the White House lawn. The tradition was started by First Lady Dolley Madison in 1810.

TUESDAY
April 9

Thomas Bradley becomes the first Los Angeles mayor to win a fourth term of office.

WEDNESDAY
April 10

Countdown begins for the launch of the space shuttle *Discovery* in 2 days time.

THURSDAY
April 11

Nova, the world's most powerful laser, is officially completed after 8 years of planning and construction. It can create a tiny point of light a thousand trillion times brighter than the sun!

FRIDAY
April 12

FIRST POLITICIAN IN SPACE: *Discovery* lifts off from Cape Canaveral, Florida, with a crew of 7, including Senator Edwin Jacob Garn of Utah.

SATURDAY
April 13

Katrin Dorre of East Germany wins the women's race of the first World Cup Marathon, held in Hiroshima, Japan. Finishing time: 2 hours, 33 minutes, 30 seconds.

SUNDAY
April 14

Anniversary of the sinking of the *Titanic* in 1912. • The men's race in the first World Cup Marathon is won by Ahmed Salah of Djibouti in 2 hours, 8 minutes, 9 seconds—the second fastest marathon time ever.

MONDAY
April 15

The Boston Marathon is won by Geoff Smith of Great Britain (time: 2 hours, 14 minutes, 5 seconds) and Lisa Larsen Werdenbach of Battle Creek, Michigan (time: 2 hours, 34 minutes, 6 seconds).

FUN FACT '85

Thomas Jefferson had a pet mockingbird that would hop after him and sit on his shoulder.

TUESDAY
April 16

Two shuttle astronauts go for a 3-hour space walk. They attach tools that look like flyswatters to the end of *Discovery*'s robot arm in an attempt to rescue a satellite that failed to go into orbit on Saturday.

WEDNESDAY
April 17

The U.S. Postal Service issues a new Love series stamp in a special ceremony in Hollywood, California. The cast members of TV's *Love Boat* are there.

THURSDAY
April 18

A miner who was trapped for 37 hours inside a mining machine buried by tons of rock is rescued by his coworkers in Palisades, Colorado.

FRIDAY
April 19

Space shuttle *Discovery* suffers minor damage when the brakes lock and a tire blows out during landing at Kennedy Space Center. It is also 90 minutes late touching down because of rain.

SATURDAY
April 20

FASTEST CHEF IN THE WEST: In Colorado, 40 chefs compete in the Grand Marnier Chefs' Ski Race on Copper Mountain.

SUNDAY
April 21

In New Jersey, Greenpeace members are charged with disorderly conduct for trying to plug up an underwater pipeline that dumps chemical wastes into the ocean.

MONDAY
April 22

Earth Day, first celebrated in 1970 • On this day in 1823, R. J. Tyers obtained a patent for roller skates.

TUESDAY
April 23

SODA SHOCKER! The Coca-Cola Company stuns America when it announces it is changing the 99-year-old recipe for Coke. The "new" Coke will be sweeter, to appeal to the taste buds of the nation's youth.

WEDNESDAY
April 24

Pope John Paul II names 28 new cardinals. • A painting by Vincent Van Gogh called *Landscape with Rising Sun* is sold for $9,900,000 in New York City—a record amount for an Impressionist painting.

COKE GOES CRAZY

That's what people think when the company announces on April 23, 1985, that they are changing Coke's traditional 99-year-old flavor. The news so shocks America that more people are aware of the Coke flavor change than were aware of the astronauts' first walk on the moon in 1969! Coca-Cola's headquarters in Atlanta is swamped with angry telegrams, letters, and nearly 40,000 telephone calls.

People call the company's new Coke "lacking in zing" and "a Coke for wimps." Old Coke clubs even spring up around the U.S. as people hoard old Coke supplies and lobby for the return of their favorite beverage.

Finally, on July 10, Coca-Cola admits it has made a mistake, and old Coke is back in. Americans celebrate by going out and buying—guess what? Coca-Cola Classic!

WHO ELSE WAS BORN IN APRIL?
THOMAS JEFFERSON

Politician, educator, scholar, architect
Jefferson was the 3d president of the U.S., and
founder of the University of Virginia.
BORN April 13, 1743, in Shadwell, Virginia

THURSDAY
April 25

Big River, a musical based on *The Adventures of Huckleberry Finn* by Mark Twain, opens in New York City.

FRIDAY
April 26

Arbor Day • It is also Bird Day and the 100th anniversary of the birth of John James Audubon, the famous ornithologist and illustrator of wildlife. The American Museum of Natural History in New York City marks the day with a new exhibit called "Audubon: Science into Art."

SATURDAY
April 27

The 8th annual World Championship Cow Chip Contest is won by Leland Searcy, with a 177-foot, 9-inch toss, in Beaver, Oklahoma.

SUNDAY
April 28

The world's largest sand castle is built in Treasure Island, Florida, using 3,500 tons of sand. • In Anaheim, California, Sabino Juarez wins a Cadillac for being 1985's three millionth visitor to Disneyland.

MONDAY
April 29

Emperor Hirohito of Japan is 84 today. • The space shuttle *Challenger* takes off from Cape Canaveral, Florida, with a crew of 7, including scientists from the Netherlands. Also on board are 2 dozen rats and a pair of squirrel monkeys!

TUESDAY
April 30

Richard Bass, a 55-year-old geologist and cattle rancher from Dallas, Texas, reaches the top of Mount Everest, making him the oldest person ever to climb the tallest mountain in the world.

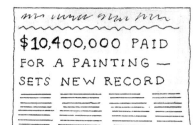

$10,400,000 PAID FOR A PAINTING — SETS NEW RECORD

NATION CELEBRATES 10th ANNIVERSARY OF THE END OF THE VIETNAM WAR

CHICAGO
DISASTER!
COKE COMPANY CHANGES FLAVOR OF 99-YEAR-OLD SODA POP

May

*M*ay comes from Maia, who was the Roman goddess of growth, increase, and blossoming.

BIRTHSTONE *Emerald*

WEDNESDAY
May 1

A team of Texas bird-watchers sets a new U.S. "birdathon" record by identifying 244 birds in 24 hours. • Residents of Sidney, Montana, line the banks of the Yellowstone River to watch for the appearance of Peter Paddlefish, a good omen for fishermen.

THURSDAY
May 2

Aboard *Challenger*, one of the squirrel monkeys that has been "space sick" is reported to be better today.

FRIDAY
May 3

COLA PANIC: People all over America are hoarding stockpiles of original-flavored Coke.

SATURDAY
May 4

Full Moon

The 111th Kentucky Derby is won by Spend a Buck. • Dr. Keith Holland, a dentist in Switzerland, Florida, announces that he has found the wreck of a 173-foot-long Civil War ship at the bottom of the St. Johns River in Florida.

SUNDAY
May 5

International Tuba Day • Thousands of boats crowd Chesapeake Bay to celebrate the first visit of *Queen Elizabeth II*, the British luxury ocean liner, to the U.S.

MONDAY
May 6

PERFECT LANDING: Space shuttle *Challenger* returns, touching down at Edwards Air Force Base in California.

TUESDAY
May 7

The Coca-Cola Company announces that it has invented a can for use in outer space. It is designed so that sodas will not lose their fizz at zero gravity. • Baseball-sized hailstones fall in Dallas, Texas!

WEDNESDAY
May 8

The Harry S Truman Good Neighbor Award is given to Ambassador Kenneth Taylor of Canada, the first non-American ever to receive the award. Taylor helped 6 Americans escape from Iran during the 1979 hostage crisis.

THURSDAY
May 9

According to a *My Weekly Reader* poll, 46 percent of the kids in grades 4 through 6 want a woman to be president of the United States.

WHO ELSE WAS BORN IN MAY?
SIGMUND FREUD

The most famous psychiatrist in history
He was the founder of psychoanalysis.
BORN May 6, 1856, in Vienna, Austria

FRIDAY
May 10

New Coke hits the shelves in stores all over the country.

SATURDAY
May 11

The ice on the Nenana River in Nenana, Alaska, breaks up at 2:36 P.M. There are 9 winning tickets in the 70th annual lottery to guess the time the ice will break. Number of tickets sold this year: 187,000.

SUNDAY
May 12

Mother's Day • In Sacramento, California, 4,000,000 bees swarm over a freeway when a truck trailer carrying hives overturns.

MONDAY
May 13

Singer and songwriter Stevie Wonder is given a special citation by the United Nations for speaking out against apartheid in South Africa.

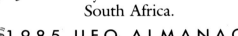

1985 UFO ALMANAC

In 1985, there are at least 3 sightings of unidentified flying objects, or UFOs. UFO sightings are nothing new. The ancient Romans re-corded seeing them, and throughout the Middle Ages, there were tales of mysterious objects and lights in the sky.

SOME UFO SIGHTINGS

March 27, 1897   Large object in Topeka, Kansas. • February 9, 1913   Group of UFOs is seen in Canada, Bermuda, Brazil, and Africa. • June 24, 1947   Flying saucer near Mount Rainier in Washington. • September 19, 1961   Man and woman picked up by UFO in New Hampshire. • September 20, 1977   UFO sighting in Leningrad in the USSR. • January 30, 1985   UFO sightings in the USSR. • March 24, 1985   UFO/fireball is sighted by people from Tennessee to Florida. • May 27, 1985   Bright white UFOs in Rockport, Texas.

TUESDAY
May 14

In Woolwich, Michigan, a veterinarian has to untangle a half-dozen young squirrels that got their tails in a knot!

WEDNESDAY
May 15

Scientists announce the discovery of the oldest dinosaur skeleton ever found. Unearthed in the Painted Desert of Arizona, the 8-foot-long skeleton is believed to be 225,000,000 years old—about 3,000,000 years older than any other dinosaur fossil known to man.

THURSDAY
May 16

The remains of the oldest known leech have been found in Waukesha County, Wisconsin. Scientists found the fossil in rocks 430,000,000 years old.

FRIDAY
May 17

United Airlines pilots go on strike. • Les Anderson catches the biggest chinook salmon on record—97 pounds 4 ounces—in the Kenai River in Alaska.

SATURDAY
May 18

The Preakness Stakes is won by a horse named Tank's Prospect, ridden by jockey Pat Day.

SUNDAY
May 19

Bird-watchers in northern Vermont spot a pair of rare peregrine falcons. • On this day in 1928, the first annual Frog Jumping Jubilee was held in Calaveras County, California.

MONDAY
May 20

The FBI arrests a suspected father-and-son spy team: retired U.S. Navy officer John Walker and his son Michael, a U.S. Navy seaman. They are charged with espionage.

TUESDAY
May 21

Scientists fly into the crater of Mount St. Helens to investigate signs of a possible eruption. • An English teacher in Orange, California, gives birth to septuplets, the largest multiple birth on record in the U.S.

WEDNESDAY
May 22

The Second Great International Paper Airplane Contest begins at the Museum of Flight in Seattle, Washington. There are more than 3,000 entries, including a flying Superman and an F-14 fighter jet from Japan.

1985 AWARDS BOARD

Nobel Peace Prize: International Physicians for the Prevention of Nuclear War
National Teacher of the Year: Theresa K. Dozier
National Spelling Bee Champion: Balu Natarajan
Best Movie (Academy Award): *Out of Africa*
Best Special Visual Effects (Academy Award): *Cocoon*
Grammy Award (album): Phil Collins, *No Jacket Required*
Grammy Award (single): USA for Africa, "We Are the World"
Male Athlete of the Year: Dwight Gooden, baseball
Female Athlete of the Year: Nancy Lopez, golf
Horse of the Year: Spend a Buck
Newbery Medal for Children's Literature: *The Hero and the Crown* by
   Robin McKinley
Caldecott Medal for Illustration: *St. George and the Dragon*, illustrated by
   Trina Schart Hyman
Best Television Comedy Series (Emmy): *The Cosby Show*

THURSDAY
May 23

Kids in North Adams, Massachusetts, picket in front of an ice-cream truck to protest high prices.

FRIDAY
May 24

Actress Jody Foster graduates from Yale University. • The Coca-Cola Company is getting about 1,500 telephone calls a day from upset Coke drinkers who want the old Coke back!

SATURDAY
May 25

Devastating cyclone hits Bangladesh, causing a one-story-high tidal wave.

SUNDAY
May 26

The Indianapolis 500 is won by Danny Sullivan, even though he spun out of control during the race and just missed smashing into a concrete wall!

MONDAY
May 27

Memorial Day • Spend a Buck wins the largest amount ever in a horse race—$2,600,000—at the Jersey Derby in Cherry Hill, New Jersey. • UFOs (bright white objects with red rings) sighted in Rockport, Texas.

FUN FACT '85

Peregrine falcons are thought to be the fastest birds in the world; they can reach a speed of 212 miles per hour when diving!

TUESDAY
May 28

PREHISTORIC MUD BALLS: The townspeople of Gill, Massachusetts, gather at a meeting to try to keep officials from destroying a stone cable which contains extremely rare, armored mud balls that may be 180,000,000 years old!

WEDNESDAY
May 29

The world's first nuclear-powered submarine, the U.S.S. *Nautilus*, launched in 1954, leaves San Francisco. It is being towed to Groton, Connecticut, to become a floating museum.

THURSDAY
May 30

The Edmonton Oilers win ice hockey's Stanley Cup, defeating the Philadelphia Flyers, 4 games to 1. • Lava is quietly oozing out of Mount St. Helens, puzzling scientists.

FRIDAY
May 31

In Pennsylvania, Ohio, and New York, a storm system with winds of 300 miles per hour spawns 41 killer tornadoes.

SOCCER RIOT IN BRUSSELS, BELGIUM— BRITISH FANS ATTACK ITALIANS

MARGARET HAMILTON, THE WICKED WITCH OF THE WEST, DIES AT AGE 82

June

June is named for the Latin *juniores*, meaning "youths," or from the Roman goddess Juno.

BIRTHSTONE *Pearl*

SATURDAY
June 1

Beginning of National Adopt-a-Cat Month and Teacher "Thank You" Week.

SUNDAY
June 2

More than 400 astronomers from around the world gather in Charlottesville, Virginia, for the 166th annual American Astronomical Society Meeting.

MONDAY
June 3
Full Moon

A 620-pound whistle is blown at South Street Seaport in New York City to mark the 50th anniversary of the maiden voyage of the *Normandie*, the largest and fastest ocean liner in existence in 1935. The whistle is from the original boat, which sank during a fire at a Hudson River pier in 1942.

TUESDAY
June 4

SCARE-OWLS? Officials at the open-air Tanglewood Music Center in Lenox, Massachusetts, who have been trying to shoo away a flock of pesky starlings, have finally succeeded—with the help of 24 inflatable owls! • It's the third day of record-breaking heat in the Southwest.

WEDNESDAY
June 5

The 58th annual National Spelling Bee begins in Washington, D.C. A barbecue is held for the finalists from 44 states who are competing for the $1,000 first prize.

THURSDAY
June 6

Scientists at the University of California in Berkeley have confirmed that there is a black hole—an object 4,000,000 times the mass of the sun—in the center of the Milky Way. • Balu Natarajan, 13, of Bolingbrook, Illinois, wins the National Spelling Bee. Winning word: *milieu*.

FRIDAY
June 7

The Bowdoin College Museum of Art in Brunswick, Maine, has commissioned 2 artists to make a sculpture out of a ton of potatoes.

SATURDAY
June 8

The Belmont Stakes horse race is won by Creme Fraiche.
• The Soviet Union is sending a giant icebreaker to free one of its research vessels, which is trapped in a huge piece of ice in Antarctica.

SUNDAY
June 9

The Los Angeles Lakers beat the Boston Celtics in the NBA championship. • In Brooklyn, New York, the first Bob Joseph Picnic is held. Thirty-six Bob Josephs (including one Roberta) come to enjoy the one-mile Bob-a-thon, the apple Bob, and shish-ke-Bob cooked on a Bob-a-que!

MONDAY
June 10

National Little League Baseball Week • A cargo jet filled with food, medicine, and clothing, bought with money made from the "We Are the World" hit single and album, leaves Los Angeles on its way to Ethiopia and the Sudan.

TUESDAY
June 11

Scientists at NASA's Jet Propulsion Laboratory in Pasadena, California, pick up signals from the Soviet space probe that has just entered the atmosphere of Venus.

WEDNESDAY
June 12

President Reagan welcomes Prime Minister Rajiv Gandhi of India to Washington, D.C., for a 4-day visit. • Vice President George Bush celebrates his 61st birthday with a white-chocolate mousse cake at a party in the White House.

THURSDAY
June 13

At the Kunsthans Museum in Zurich, Switzerland, a man sets fire to a painting by Peter Paul Rubens worth $1,900,000. • In London, a gold penny from the time of King Henry III (dated 1257) breaks an auction record by selling for $91,500!

FUN FACT '85

Cocker spaniels get their name from their original purpose, which was to hunt woodcocks.

FRIDAY
June 14

Flag Day • Argentina announces it will be using a new currency called the *austral*, which will be a thousand times greater in value than the peso it replaces.

SATURDAY
June 15

Smile Power Day • Soviet probe *Vega 1* lands on the dark side of Venus and begins drilling into the hot soil (840°F) to discover what it contains.

SUNDAY
June 16

Father's Day • Great Britain's Steve Cram wins the 1,500-meter race in France by a mere four hundredths of a second, setting a new world record. • In Birmingham, Michigan, Andy North wins the U.S. Open golf championship by one stroke!

WHO ELSE WAS BORN IN JUNE?
HELEN KELLER

Author and lecturer
Blind and deaf from the age of 2, she nevertheless
learned to read, write, and speak, and she graduated
from Radcliffe College with honors. She published 2
books, *The Story of My Life* and *Helen Keller's
Journal*.
BORN June 27, 1880, in Tuscumbia, Alabama

MONDAY
June 17

Space shuttle *Discovery* is launched from Cape Canaveral in
Florida with the first Arab astronaut as part of the crew.

TUESDAY
June 18

HEAT WAVE: It's 88°F in Seattle, Washington—
18 degrees above normal. It's 113°F in Las Vegas, Nevada.
In California, apricots are getting sunburned.

WEDNESDAY.
June 19

National Fink Week • Pentagon scientists try to bounce a laser
beam from earth off *Discovery* for a Star Wars defense systems
test, but they fail. It turns out ground controllers sent the
instructions in miles instead of in feet!

THURSDAY
June 20

A house dating back to 1800 B.C. is discovered by
archaeologists in an excavation in Kalamazoo, Michigan.

FRIDAY
June 21

Summer solstice. Summer begins at exactly 6:44 P.M.
(EDT). • The Star Wars test succeeds: A laser beam from
earth is bounced off an 8-inch mirror mounted on space shuttle
Discovery.

SATURDAY
June 22

JungleWorld opens at New York City's Bronx Zoo. An indoor
re-creation of the tropical lands of southern Asia, it has rain
forests, crocodiles, monkeys swinging from vines, and
Junglelab: a classroom in the treetops made to resemble a
research station.

ARAB PRINCE BECOMES ASTRONAUT

On June 17, space shuttle *Discovery* blasts off from Cape Canaveral at 7:33
A.M. On board is the first Arab astronaut, Prince Sultan bin Salman ibn Abdul
Aziz al-Saud, nephew of King Fahd of Saudi Arabia. He has received special
permission to pray without the usual ritual washings and will observe the new
moon, which marks the end of Ramadan, the Muslim month of fasting.

SUNDAY
June 23

King Fahd telephones his nephew on board the space shuttle *Discovery*. • In Philadelphia, Pennsylvania, Eric Heiden, a 5-time Olympic gold medalist in speed skating, wins the first CoreStates United States Professional Cycling Road Championship by 5 yards.

MONDAY
June 24

Discovery lands at Edwards Air Force Base in California. • In London, the 99th Wimbledon tennis championships are postponed a day because of torrential rain.

TUESDAY
June 25

COLA WARS: The Pepsi-Cola Company announces that it has, like Coca-Cola, developed its own "space can" for the astronauts to drink from on their July 12 shuttle flight. • In Hallett, Oklahoma, a fireworks plant explodes.

WEDNESDAY
June 26

Happy birthday! The United Nations is 40 today. • Scientists at the National Zoo in Washington, D.C., are hoping that pandas Ling-Ling and Hsing-Hsing will mate.

THURSDAY
June 27

The U.S. military conducts a secret experiment by setting off 4,880 tons of high explosives in New Mexico, the largest explosion ever created except for the atomic bomb.

FRIDAY
June 28

CHIMP CHAT: Kanzi, a pygmy chimpanzee in Atlanta, Georgia, has been taught to talk by pressing symbols on a keyboard.

SATURDAY
June 29

Shigechiyo Izumi, believed to be the world's oldest man, celebrates his 120th birthday in Japan. • The Beatles' psychedelic-yellow Rolls Royce is sold for $2,229,000 in New York City.

SUNDAY
June 30

A new Basketball Hall of Fame opens in Springfield, Massachusetts. • In Raleigh, Mississippi, Jeff "Faucet Man" Barber wins the 31t National Tobacco-spitting Contest.

TWA JET HIJACKED TO BERUIT BY TERRORISTS

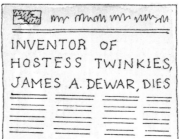

INVENTOR OF HOSTESS TWINKIES, JAMES A. DEWAR, DIES

RAJIV GANDHI, PRIME MINISTER OF INDIA, VISITS U.S.

July

*T*his month was named to honor Julius Caesar.

BIRTHSTONE *Ruby*

MONDAY
July 1

Trainers at Gulf World in Panama City, Florida, try to get a mother whale to nurse her baby. The whales were rescued after they got washed ashore 5 miles apart.

TUESDAY
July 2
Full Moon

The European Space Agency launches Europe's first interplanetary probe, the *Giotto*, which will rendezvous with Halley's comet next year on March 13.

WEDNESDAY
July 3

Back to the Future, a movie about a boy who travels back in time and meets his parents when they were kids, opens in movie theaters across the country. It stars Michael J. Fox.

THURSDAY
July 4

Independence Day • Oscar Rodriguez, age 21, wins the annual Nathan's Fourth of July Hot-Dog Eating Contest in Coney Island, New York, by wolfing down 11¾ dogs in 12 minutes.

FRIDAY
July 5

The first nuclear-powered submarine, the U.S.S. *Nautilus*, returns to Groton, Connecticut, and is welcomed with fireworks and thousands of balloons.

SATURDAY
July 6

Martina Navratilova beats Chris Evert Lloyd in the women's finals at the Wimbledon tennis championships. It's the fourth year in a row that Navratilova has won at Wimbledon.

SUNDAY
July 7

Boris Becker, age 17, beats Kevin Curren in the men's finals and becomes the youngest tennis player to win a singles title at Wimbledon. • In Mashpee, Massachusetts, the Wampanoag Indians hold their 50th annual powwow.

MONDAY
July 8

Disney announces its plans to build a new movie and television theme park near Disney World in Florida. • A major forest fire is burning near San Luis Obispo in California.

TUESDAY
July 9

Scientists from the New England Aquarium in Boston say they have discovered the calving grounds of the northern right whale near the coasts of Florida and Georgia. Only about 300 of these rare whales exist in the world.

WHO ELSE WAS BORN IN JULY?
RAFFI (RAFFI CAVOUKIAN)

Canadian singer and songwriter; popular children's
performer since 1974
He is best known for his 1976 album, *Singable Songs
for the Very Young*.
BORN July 8, 1948, in Cairo, Egypt

WEDNESDAY
July 10

The Coca-Cola Company announces that it is bringing back
the original formula Coke, to be called Coca-Cola Classic.
Since the new Coke went on sale in April, the company has
received more than 40,000 phone calls from customers
demanding the old Coke.

THURSDAY
July 11

Nolan Ryan of baseball's Houston Astros becomes the first
pitcher in a major-league team to strike out 4,000 batters.
• Two patas monkeys escape from the San Francisco Zoo.

FRIDAY
July 12

Space shuttle *Challenger*'s launch is called off 3 seconds
before liftoff because of a failure in the booster rockets.
• Opening day of the annual Chicken Show in Wayne,
Nebraska, featuring the National Cluck-off Tournament.

SATURDAY
July 13

About 1,500,000,000 people in 152 countries watch the Live
Aid concert—which takes place in London, England, and in
Philadelphia, Pennsylvania—on television. The 16-hour concert
raises $75,100,000 for starving people in Africa.

SUNDAY
July 14

Mist, a cow in Montpelier, Vermont, has been sold for
$1,300,000, the highest price ever paid for a cow. • Dr.
Sanford Stein, a dentist in Rumson, New Jersey, has invented
a night brace for Cabbage Patch dolls! He's sold 2,500 so far.

MONDAY
July 15

In Kenya, 12,000 women attend the United Nations Decade
for Women Conference. • Weekend rain has helped 11,055
fire fighters slow more than 400 fires that have been burning
throughout the western U.S.

FUN FACT '85

The world's first vacuum cleaner was so
big it had to be moved on a cart pulled by 2 men.

TUESDAY
July 16

Baseball's All-Star Game is won by the National League, 6-1. • At the World Hot-Air Balloon Championships in Battle Creek, Michigan, 2 balloons collide in midair!

WEDNESDAY
July 17

National Space Week • NASA's first made-in-space product goes on sale today: tiny, perfectly round plastic beads.

THURSDAY
July 18

Poisonous black widow spiders are turning up in dashboard parts in a Saline, Michigan, automobile plant! They were transported from a manufacturing plant in Mexico.

FRIDAY
July 19

Sharon Christa McAuliffe from Concord, New Hampshire, is chosen to be the first private-citizen passenger in space. She was picked out of 11,000 applicants to fly on a future shuttle mission.

SATURDAY
July 20

Treasure hunter Mel Fisher and a team of divers find the wreckage of a Spanish ship, the *Nuestra Señora de Atocha*, which sank in 1622 near Key West, Florida. The wreck contains 47 *tons* of gold and silver worth $400,000,000, making it the greatest treasure ever found.

SUNDAY
July 21

In Pittsburgh, Pennsylvania, 8,500 steelworkers go on strike, the first major steel strike since 1959.

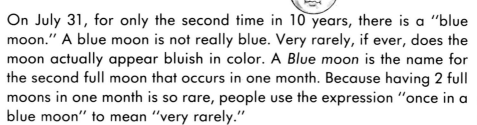

ONCE IN A BLUE MOON

On July 31, for only the second time in 10 years, there is a "blue moon." A blue moon is not really blue. Very rarely, if ever, does the moon actually appear bluish in color. A *Blue moon* is the name for the second full moon that occurs in one month. Because having 2 full moons in one month is so rare, people use the expression "once in a blue moon" to mean "very rarely."

MONDAY
July 22

Troop 471 of Somerset, Pennsylvania, begins its week-long Boy Scout Jamboree at Fort A. P. Hill in Virginia.

TUESDAY
July 23

A horse named Seattle Dancer is sold in Lexington, Kentucky, for $13,100,000, the highest amount ever paid for a horse.

WEDNESDAY
July 24

Scientists are baffled by a strange alga that is growing so fast it has turned the water in some Long Island bays completely brown. • Bob, 1985's first hurricane, comes ashore in South Carolina.

THURSDAY *July 25*	Two monkeys that escaped from the San Francisco Zoo have been spotted lounging in the backyard trees of the West Portal neighborhood. Zoo keepers hope to lure the monkeys back with Monkey Chow.
FRIDAY *July 26*	The Soviet research ship *Mikhail Somov* and its crew are freed today after being trapped for 133 days in Antarctic ice.
SATURDAY *July 27*	A bee hunt is on in central California for the South American "killer" bees that have been spotted for the first time in the U.S.
SUNDAY *July 28*	President Li Xiannian of China meets Mickey Mouse at Disneyland in California. The president has been in the U.S. since Tuesday.

WHAT'S HOT IN 1985

Coca-Cola Classic	Gummy Bears	*Back to the Future*
Jellybeans	Rambo	Dwight Gooden
Earrings for boys	Telescopes	The sixties
Madonna	CD players	Wham!
The Statue of Liberty	Halley's comet	Plastic chain-link necklaces
Dove Bars	Bubble Yum	Talking teddy bears
Diet chocolate soda pop	Bruce Springsteen	

MONDAY *July 29*	Space shuttle *Challenger* is launched from Cape Canaveral in Florida and achieves orbit, even though one of its main engines fails 5 minutes after takeoff.
TUESDAY *July 30*	A worm named Betty wins the Southwest Branch Library Worm Race in Green Bay, Wisconsin. The winning worm, beat 19 other worms, including Mr. Fat Man and Speedy.
WEDNESDAY *July 31* Blue Moon	**UNINVITED GUESTS:** Hordes of wild Canada geese in Greenwich, Connecticut, are chasing bicyclists, snatching food from picnickers, and swimming in private pools!

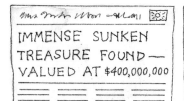

IMMENSE SUNKEN TREASURE FOUND — VALUED AT $400,000,000

COCA-COLA BRINGS BACK OLD COKE — FANS ELATED

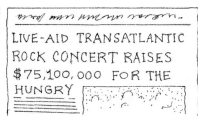

LIVE-AID TRANSATLANTIC ROCK CONCERT RAISES $75,100,000 FOR THE HUNGRY

August

August was named in honor of Roman emperor Augustus, whose lucky month it was.

BIRTHSTONE *Peridot*

THURSDAY
August 1

August 1 to 7 is National Clown Week.
• The U.S. Congress goes on vacation.

FRIDAY
August 2

Two Soviet cosmonauts go for a 5-hour space walk to put new power cells in the *Salyut 7* space station. • A brutal thunderstorm in Cheyenne, Wyoming (6 inches of rain in less than 4 hours), causes flooding.

SATURDAY
August 3

SHARK WATCH: Sharks are reported to be plentiful this season up and down the shores of Long Island, New York. • In Wilmington, Delaware, the Munchkins of Oz Convention begins, and the National Hobo Convention takes place in Britt, Iowa.

SUNDAY
August 4

Two mild earthquakes rumble in Coalinga, California.
• A buffalo attacks a Buick in Louisburg, North Carolina.

MONDAY
August 5

Space shuttle *Challenger* beams down to earth amazing pictures of the sun's surface, which have been taken with an instrument called the Solar Optical Universal Polarimeter.

TUESDAY
August 6

Major league baseball players go on strike. • *Challenger* lands at Edwards Air Force Base in California. • NASA announces plans to take chicken eggs into space!

WEDNESDAY
August 7

In California, Marin County officials report that an annoying humming noise people have been complaining about is actually the mating call of the male singing toadfish.

THURSDAY
August 8

Baseball players are back in the ballparks—the strike is over! • In St. Louis, Missouri, the largest indoor shopping mall in America opens with a gala celebration attended by 40,000 people and featuring 30,000 balloons and 400 homing pigeons.

FRIDAY
August 9

Singer Bruce Springsteen performs to an audience of 70,000 in Chicago, Illinois, as part of a 15-month international tour.

SATURDAY
August 10

TV talk show host Johnny Carson dives for sunken treasure at the site of the *Nuestra Señora de Atocha*. The dive is filmed by *National Geographic Magazine*.

SUNDAY
August 11

The Perseid meteor shower is highly visible tonight with about 70 white, yellow, green, and orange streaks of light an hour.

MONDAY
August 12

ZOO NEWS: Officials of the Los Angeles Zoo announce the birth of a rare Indian rhinoceros named Chandra. Meanwhile, Ayers, a koala bear from the San Diego Zoo, arrives in Milwaukee, Wisconsin, for a 30-day visit and is greeted with a fanfare of 1,000 balloons and the Great Lakes Navy Band.

TUESDAY
August 13

Peter Johnson from Texas swims the English Channel in 8 hours, 20 minutes—14 minutes faster than last year's record!

WEDNESDAY
August 14

Thomas Greene from Maryland eats 2.2 pounds of snails in just 2 minutes 43.95 seconds, and wins the Champion Snail Eater title.

MONKEYING AROUND

The monkeys at the San Diego Zoo are clever about escape plans. On August 13, orangutan Ken Allen scales his enclosure, finds a crowbar, and drops it to his roommate, Vicky, who pops open the front glass of the exhibit! They are caught before they can escape.

THURSDAY
August 15

Hurricane Danny crosses the Gulf of Mexico.
• The Smithsonian Institution's Dial-a-Phenomenon line is already getting 4,000 to 5,000 calls a week. It has been set up to answer questions about viewing Halley's comet.

FRIDAY
August 16

Madonna marries actor Sean Penn today, her 26th birthday. • Radio station KFDI in Wichita, Kansas, has created what may be the world's largest scarecrow: It's 32-feet-high and is made with 30 bales of hay.

SATURDAY
August 17

Four Madagascar ground boas hatch at the Fresno Zoo in California, the first successful breeding of this kind of snake north of the equator.

SUNDAY
August 18

Student stuntman Steve Trotter from Rhode Island goes over Niagara Falls in a pickle barrel. He's the 7th person in 84 years to survive the stunt.

WHO ELSE WAS BORN IN AUGUST?
NEIL ARMSTRONG

U.S. astronaut
On July 20, 1969, he became the first man to set
foot on the moon, during a mission in the *Apollo II*
module.
BORN August 5, 1930, in Wapakoneta, Ohio

MONDAY
August 19

Robert E. Barber breaks the speed record for a steam car,
going 145.607 miles per hour at Bonneville Salt Flats in Utah.

TUESDAY
August 20

NASA announces its plans for the first totally automated
factory in space, to be built by a company in Houston, Texas.

WEDNESDAY
August 21

Koko, the "talking" gorilla, who became famous for having
cried when she was told that her pet cat All Ball died,
now has two new cat friends, Lips and Smokey.

THURSDAY
August 22

Koala Crossing opens at the San Francisco Zoo in California.
• In New York, the largest lottery jackpot in history,
$41,000,000, is won by 3 tickets. One of the
tickets is shared by 21 coworkers.

FUN FACT '85

On August 24, 1985, at 9:52 A.M., Disneyland
receives its 250 millionth visitor.

FRIDAY
August 23

A robot that is programmed to stop criminals is stolen from a
home in Arlington, Virginia, while its owners are on vacation!

SATURDAY
August 24

A team from Seoul in South Korea wins the 39th annual Little
League World Series in Williamsport, Pennsylvania.

SUNDAY
August 25

The New York Mets' Dwight Gooden, age 20,
becomes the youngest major league baseball
pitcher to win 20 games in one season.

MONDAY
August 26

RESCUED: Three Dutch balloonists trying to set a new record
for crossing the Atlantic crash into the ocean 900 miles west of
England and are saved by a passing merchant ship.

THE HURRICANES OF 1985

In 1985, the U.S. has more hurricanes (6) than in any year since 1916. During the hurricane season (July to November), parts of every coastal state receive hurricane warnings!

A hurricane is a severe storm that originates over tropical waters and has winds of 74, or more miles per hour.

- **Bob** moves across South Carolina on July 25.
- **Danny** reaches Louisiana on August 15.
- ***Elena** hits Biloxi, Mississippi, on September 2.
- ***Gloria** is east of the Bahamas on September 25; entire U.S. coast gets hurricane warning. The storm hits North Carolina on September 26 and the New York Metropolitan area on September 27.
- **Juan** hits New Orleans, Louisiana, on October 28; and then Pensacola, Florida, on October 31.
- **Kate** hits the Florida panhandle on November 21.

*Major hurricanes.

TUESDAY
August 27

Space shuttle *Discovery* lifts off from Cape Canaveral in Florida. Mission: To launch 3 new satellites, retrieve and repair another satellite, and take movies for a film to be called *The Dream Is Alive*.

WEDNESDAY
August 28

The president of Cartier stomps on and crushes 25,000 pairs of counterfeit Ferrari sunglasses in New York City to make a point about the problem he is having with people making fakes of his company's product.

THURSDAY
August 29

Bill Cosby and former President Jimmy Carter film a TV special in Atlanta, Georgia, called "Kids Just Want to Have Fun," a program warning children about the dangers of smoking and drinking.

FRIDAY
August 30

Full Moon

A state of emergency is declared in 24 counties along the coast of the Gulf of Mexico as Hurricane Elena advances with winds of up to 125 miles per hour.

SATURDAY
August 31

Astronauts William Fisher and James Van Hoften take a 7-hour-1-minute-long space walk—a U.S. record!

JAPANESE JETLINER CRASHES IN WORST SINGLE PLANE ACCIDENT IN HISTORY

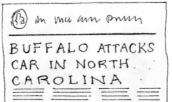

BUFFALO ATTACKS CAR IN NORTH CAROLINA

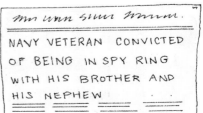

NAVY VETERAN CONVICTED OF BEING IN SPY RING WITH HIS BROTHER AND HIS NEPHEW

September

*T*he name September comes from the Latin *septem*, meaning "seven." This was the seventh month of the old Roman calendar.

BIRTHSTONE *Sapphire*

SUNDAY
September 1

French and American explorers find the wreck of the *Titanic*, which sank in 1912, 560 miles off the coast of Newfoundland. • A screwdriver accidentally floats out of the space shuttle *Discovery* and into orbit.

MONDAY
September 2

Labor Day • Hurricane Elena blows into Mississippi. Twenty-one dolphins are evacuated from Marine Life Aquarium to the swimming pools of 3 local hotels in Gulfport, Mississippi.

TUESDAY
September 3

In New York City's Central Park, world-champion hang glider John Pendry, who holds the long-distance record of 187 miles, gives a demonstration in a 30-foot, yellow-and-white hang glider.

WEDNESDAY
September 4

POTATO GLUT: The potato crop is so plentiful, farmers are getting only 42 cents for a 10-pound bag!

THURSDAY
September 5

The discoverers of the sunken wreck of the *Titanic* head home with thousands of photographs, hours of videotape—and 5 cases of wine, found in the wreckage.

FRIDAY
September 6

Great Plains Huff 'n' Puff Balloon Races in Topeka, Kansas. • The National Championship Indian Powwow begins in Grand Prairie, Texas, with dance contests, an Indian arts and crafts show, and a tepee competition.

SATURDAY
September 7

Hana Mandlikova of Czechoslovakia wins the women's singles competition in the U.S. Open tennis championships.

SUNDAY
September 8

Grandparents' Day • The men's singles competition at the U.S. Open tennis championships is won by Ivan Lendl of Czechoslovakia.

WHO ELSE WAS BORN IN SEPTEMBER? JOHNNY APPLESEED (BORN JOHN CHAPMAN)

Pioneer and U.S. folk hero
Chapman got his nickname because he spent about 40 years traveling around—mostly in the Ohio River region—planting and tending apple orchards as well as giving out seedlings to pioneers.
BORN September 26, 1774, in Leominster, Massachusetts

MONDAY
September 9

The triumphant researchers who found the *Titanic* arrive at their home port of Woods Hole, Massachusetts, and are greeted by cheering crowds, balloons, and airhorns.

TUESDAY
September 10

National Rub-a-Bald-Head Week • A 50-year-old Frenchman, Yvol Le Caer, pedals more than 60 miles across the English Channel on an aquabicycle, in just under 17 hours.

WEDNESDAY
September 11

CLOSE ENCOUNTER WITH A COMET: A U.S. scientific satellite called the *International Cometary Explorer* flies through the tail of the comet Giacobini-Zinner, about 44,000,000 miles from earth, and sends pictures back to earth. It is the first direct probe of a comet.

THURSDAY
September 12

Ground is broken for the world's largest telescope, to be built on top of 13,600-foot Mauna Kea in Hawaii. When finished, in 1991, it will be powerful enough to detect a candle on the moon!

THE FINDING OF THE TITANIC

On September 1, a team of French and American explorers locates the famous sunken luxury liner using a sophisticated new remote-control submarine called the *Argo*. The *Titanic*, which struck an iceberg in 1912 and sank during its first voyage, lies at a depth of 12,000 feet, its hull broken in two.

The *Argo* takes hundreds of feet of videotape and 12,000 color photographs. The director of the discovery team, Robert D. Ballard, believes the extreme depth of the wreck will make it impossible to lift the ship out of the ocean. There she sank, and there she will remain.

FRIDAY
September 13

Friday the 13th. Also Blame-Someone-Else Day.

FUN FACT '85

Special Monopoly sets made during World War II and sent to prisoners of war contained secret maps of escape routes, tiny compasses, and real money.

SATURDAY
September 14

The biggest wedding cake in the world is baked in Thailand. It is 45-feet-high and has 70 tiers made with 10,000 eggs, about 530 pounds of butter, 440 pounds of flour, and 250 quarts of milk.

SUNDAY
September 15

Two fishermen hook the same 800-pound tuna in Marshfield, Massachusetts. Each one claims the fish belongs to him, leaving a judge to settle the matter.

MONDAY
September 16

First day of Rosh Hashanah. Also Muslim New Year; year 1406 of the Islamic era begins at sunset.

TUESDAY
September 17

Citizenship Day • Orders for *Titanic* model kits are up 500 percent since the famous ship was found on September 1.

WEDNESDAY
September 18

Basketball player Patrick Ewing signs a record $17,000,000 multiyear contract to play with the New York Knicks.

THURSDAY
September 19

Major earthquake devastates Mexico City in Mexico. Huge buildings crumble into ruins.

FRIDAY
September 20

Today is the Rayne Frog Festival, which features frog jumping, racing, and eating contests, in Rayne, Louisiana.

SATURDAY
September 21

Michael Spinks becomes the first light heavyweight boxer to win the heavyweight boxing championship when he beats Larry Holmes in Las Vegas, Nevada.

SUNDAY
September 22

Autumn equinox • Farm Aid, a benefit concert sponsored by singer Willie Nelson in Champaign, Illinois, raises $7,000,000 for American farmers.

MONDAY
September 23

The artist Christo's latest work of art officially "opens" today: He has wrapped the oldest bridge in Paris, France, in more than 40,000 yards of beige nylon. The material is held in place with 6 miles of rope!

SOME ENDANGERED SPECIES OF 1985

By the end of 1985, the following animals have been added to the U.S. Fish and Wildlife Service's growing list of endangered species:

Grizzly bear   Morro Bay kangaroo rat
Eastern cougar   California northern flying squirrel

TUESDAY
September 24

Jason Bunn of Great Britain wins the World Monopoly Championship in Atlantic City, New Jersey, which is held to mark the occasion of the game's 50th anniversary. The prize: $15,140—the equivalent of all the play money in a Monopoly set.

WEDNESDAY
September 25

Yom Kippur • The U.S. Postal Service issues a block of 4 stamps featuring breeds of American horses: the saddlebred, the Morgan, the Appaloosa, and the quarter horse.

THURSDAY
September 26

Hurricane Gloria hits the eastern U.S. with winds of 130 miles per hour. • Two Soviet cosmonauts, Vladimir Dzhanibekov and Georgy Grechko, return to earth from the orbiting space station *Salyut 7*.

FRIDAY
September 27

It's Kiss-a-Cop Day in Philadelphia, Pennsylvania. • Hurricane Gloria sweeps through the New York metropolitan area.

SATURDAY
September 28

A killer whale has been born at Sea World in Orlando, Florida.

SUNDAY
September 29

Full Moon

More than 115,000 people flock to Vermillion, Ohio, for the annual Woolybear Festival, the state's largest 1-day festival, a day devoted to wooly bear caterpillars. The events include the Woolybear 500—a 500-centimeter race for caterpillars.

MONDAY
September 30

A report is published in the *Journal of the American Academy of Child Psychiatry* showing that playing video games is not damaging to students. • A national survey shows that old Coke is beating new Coke, 9 to 1.

HURRICANES ELENA AND GLORIA BATTER EAST COAST

WRECK OF THE TITANIC DISCOVERED!

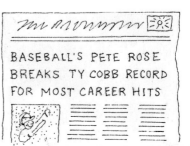

BASEBALL'S PETE ROSE BREAKS TY COBB RECORD FOR MOST CAREER HITS

October

*O*ctober was the eighth month of the old Roman calendar; the name is from the Latin *octo*, meaning "eight."

BIRTHSTONE *Opal*

TUESDAY
October 1

International Doll Collectors' Month begins.
• Today is World Vegetarian Day.

WEDNESDAY
October 2

Archaeologists examine a 350- to 1,000-year-old skull and bones that were unearthed when Hurricane Gloria knocked over a tree in Waterford, Connecticut.

THURSDAY
October 3

U.S. space shuttle *Atlantis* blasts off on its first voyage—a top-secret military mission.

FRIDAY
October 4

Chemists at the University of Chicago have found evidence that it was a worldwide fire which wiped out the dinosaurs 65,000,000 years ago: 65,000,000-year-old soot!

SATURDAY
October 5

Eddie Robinson of Grambling State University in Louisiana breaks the college-football coaching record for the most wins with the 324th football victory of his 44-year career.

SUNDAY
October 6

A 30-foot-high hammered-copper sculpture made by artist Raymond Kaskey is floated down the Willamette River on its way to its destination atop a building in Portland, Oregon.

MONDAY
October 7

Lynette Woodard, who is 5 feet 11 inches tall, is chosen to be the first woman member of the Harlem Globetrotters basketball team. • Disastrous mud slide in Ponce, Puerto Rico!

TUESDAY
October 8

Scientists are trying to preserve some 4,600-year-old air that has been trapped in an ancient burial chamber discovered near the Great Pyramid of Giza in Egypt.

WEDNESDAY
October 9

In New York City, opening ceremonies take place in Central Park for Strawberry Fields, a special garden created to honor the memory of Beatle John Lennon.

THURSDAY
October 10

The National Air and Space Museum unveils its model of a prehistoric flying reptile, the pterodactyl, which will be able to soar over the Mall in Washington, D.C., next year.

FUN FACT '85

In 1985, there are 114,427 millionaires in California.

FRIDAY
October 11

The Nobel Peace Prize committee announces that instead of going to an individual, the 1985 prize will go to a group called the International Physicians for the Prevention of Nuclear War.

SATURDAY
October 12

More than 400 parachutists jump off the 874-foot-high New River Gorge Bridge in Fayetteville, West Virginia. Almost all the jumpers scream!

SUNDAY
October 13

In Chicago, Illinois, the world's most powerful atom smasher reaches an all-time record-high level of energy; its smashing of protons and antiprotons releases 1.6 trillion volts of electricity.

MONDAY
October 14

Columbus Day • A concrete wall of a lock along the St. Lawrence Seaway collapses. Cargo ships are backed up, unable to get through to the inland waters of Canada and the U.S.

TUESDAY
October 15

INSECT EXCHANGE: The Cincinnati Zoo in Ohio sends 6 unicorn beetles and 12 velvet ants to Moscow. Russian insects are being sent to Cincinnati in return.

WEDNESDAY
October 16

Passengers in a small boat in the Sacramento River Channel near Rio Vista, California, are startled when a 45-ton, 40-foot-long humpback whale surfaces nearby. He seems lost and confused.

THURSDAY
October 17

After scientists try using sound recordings of unfriendly killer whales to scare "Humphrey," the humpback whale, toward the sea, he is left alone in hopes that he will find his own way back to the Pacific Ocean.

FRIDAY
October 18

The U.S. Mint begins making 3 different coins to commemorate the Statue of Liberty's 100th anniversary in 1986. • Vice President Bush completes a 6-day visit to China.

SATURDAY
October 19

Baseball's World Series between the Kansas City Royals and the St. Louis Cardinals opens in Kansas City, Missouri. • A typhoon hits the Philippines.

THE COMET COMMOTION

Halley's comet is the brightest of all periodic comets. It passes close to earth about every 76 years. Like all comets, it orbits the sun. In November 1985, Halley's comet passes earth on its way to the sun; it will then go around the sun and pass earth again on its way back in February 1986. The comet is named after Edmond Halley, who was the first person to figure out that it traveled in a huge orbit and not in a straight line. After the 1682 appearance, he predicted that the comet would return in 76 years—and it did!

In October and November of 1985, as the long-awaited comet draws nearer to earth, America's "comet fever" builds. More than 50 new books about the famous comet are published and hundreds of Halley's comet products and souvenirs are launched, including:

Halley's comet telescopes (Halleyscopes) • Halley's comet binoculars • Halley's comet T-shirts • Halley's comet jewelry • Halley's comet posters • Halley's comet stamps • Halley's comet dolls • Halley's comet coins • Halley's comet computer programs • Halley's comet slide sets • Halley's comet glow-in-the-dark clothing • Halley's comet picnic baskets • Halley's comet watches • Halley's comet pins • Halley's comet soap • Halley's comet perfume • Halley's comet fountain pens • Halley's comet balloons • Halley's comet Frisbees and Halley's comet pills!

SUNDAY *October 20*	In Dearborn, Michigan, the world's largest outdoor museum, the Henry Ford Museum, holds an auction of 400 antique cars and other items, including 2 railroad locomotives, 24 horse-drawn carriages, and a number of old motorcycles.
MONDAY *October 21*	Today is the 106th anniversary of the day Thomas Edison invented the electric lamp.
TUESDAY *October 22*	The Louisville Transit Authority in Kentucky has given 117-year-old Frank Smith a pass to ride the city buses free.
WEDNESDAY *October 23*	A replica of the Godspeed, the ship that carried the first permanent English settlers to America, docks in Jamestown, Virginia. The original Godspeed left England in December 1606, and arrived May 14, 1607.
THURSDAY *October 24*	DOG AUDITIONS: The Michigan Opera Theatre holds auditions for beagles at 11:00 A.M. The company needs 8 dogs, and they will be paid $3 per performance!

WHO ELSE WAS BORN IN OCTOBER?
ELEANOR ROOSEVELT

U.S. First Lady, writer, lecturer, and diplomat
The wife of President Franklin D. Roosevelt, she
was called the First Lady of the World.
BORN October 11, 1884, in New York, New York

FRIDAY
October 25

Humphrey, the humpback whale, passes under Liberty Island Bridge while marine scientists clang on submerged pipes to try to coax him along.

SATURDAY
October 26

In a special ceremony, the Australian government gives Ayers Rock in the Northern Territory back to the aborigines. The rock is 1,200 feet high.

SUNDAY
October 27

Kansas City triumphs over St. Louis to win baseball's World Series.

MONDAY
October 28

Full Moon

Hurricane Juan wreaks havoc in Louisiana, with damage of more than $1 billion. • Starting today, you can buy a 1-square-inch piece of Harlem in New York City for $5!

TUESDAY
October 29

Three garbage collectors in Baltimore, Maryland, who were fired for picking up too much trash, are back at work, with a strict warning not to go over the limit of four 20-gallon containers per business or residence.

WEDNESDAY
October 30

WORLD'S LARGEST PUMPKIN? The 531-pound Great Pumpkin arrives in New York City's Central Park. • Space shuttle *Challenger* is launched from Cape Canaveral in Florida with a crew of 8, the largest ever.

THURSDAY
October 31

Halloween • The space scientists on board *Challenger* experiment with weightlessness by taking rides on a "space sled" inside the shuttle. A fruit fly that somehow got into the spacelab module is also weightless!

TERRORISTS HIJACK
ITALIAN CRUISE SHIP
ACHILLE LAURO IN THE
MEDITERRANEAN SEA

HUMPBACK WHALE
SIGHTED IN
SACRAMENTO RIVER

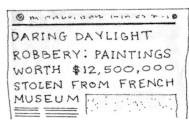

DARING DAYLIGHT
ROBBERY: PAINTINGS
WORTH $12,500,000
STOLEN FROM FRENCH
MUSEUM

November

November was the ninth month of the old Roman calendar. The name comes from the Latin *novem*, meaning "nine."

BIRTHSTONE *Topaz*

FRIDAY
November 1

On this day in 1939, the Human Torch and the Submariner first appeared in Marvel comics. • In November 1985, Cherry Coke is America's hot new soda!

SATURDAY
November 2

Hurricane Juan moves north, dumping heavy rains on West Virginia, Virginia, Maryland, and Pennsylvania.

SUNDAY
November 3

Sandwich Day, in honor of the person who invented sandwiches, the Earl of Sandwich

MONDAY
November 4

HOME SWEET HOME: Humphrey, the humpback whale, finds his way back to the Pacific Ocean after being lost for 24 days in California's Sacramento and San Joaquin rivers. He is led downstream and under the Golden Gate Bridge by a boat playing recordings underwater of whales feeding.

TUESDAY
November 5

A 48-year-old Canadian mechanic, John David Munday, goes over Niagara Falls in a barrel. He survives the 178-foot drop but has to pay a $1,500 fine the next day!

WEDNESDAY
November 6

Soviet KGB agent Vitaly Yurchenko who defected to the U.S. in July, changes his mind and returns to the Soviet Union. • Space shuttle *Challenger* lands at Edwards Air Force Base in California.

THURSDAY
November 7

President Reagan declares West Virginia a disaster area because of devastating floods. • The St. Lawrence Seaway reopens after having been closed for repairs for 3 weeks. Ships that have been waiting "rush" through the Welland Canal at the rate of one an hour!

FRIDAY
November 8

Ricky Chin of Montgomery, Texas, wins the $100,000 first prize in the Red Man All-American Bass Championship at Lake Havasu in Arizona. His total catch: 17 pounds, 10 ounces.

SATURDAY
November 9

Gary Kasparov, age 22, becomes the youngest world chess champion in history, defeating Anatoly Karpov after a record 14-month competition.

SUNDAY
November 10

On their first visit together to the U.S., Prince Charles and Princess Diana are shown around the city of Washington, D.C. A special mural of the Princess has been made out of 10,000 jellybeans!

MONDAY
November 11

BAD SPORTSMANSHIP: A fan throws a snowball onto the football field in Denver, Colorado, causing one of the San Francisco 49ers to fumble during a field-goal attempt in a game against the Denver Broncos.

TUESDAY
November 12

Prince Charles and Princess Diana fly to Palm Beach, Florida. They are greeted by Mickey Mouse, and Prince Charles joins in a game of polo.

FUN FACT '85

A group of cats is called either a *clowder* of cats or a *clutter* of cats.

WEDNESDAY
November 13

The snowcapped volcano Nevado del Ruiz erupts in Colombia. • In Spokane, Washington, Lynette Woodward plays her first game with the Harlem Globetrotters. She's the first woman on the team.

THURSDAY
November 14

At last, after 75 years, Halley's comet is clearly in view! With binoculars, it can be seen across the U.S. starting tonight at 9:00 P.M. (local time).

FRIDAY
November 15

American Enterprise Day • A dentist in New Haven, Connecticut, has been ordered by the city to take down a 4-foot-high tooth from the lawn in front of his office.

SATURDAY
November 16

President Reagan flies to Switzerland for the Geneva peace talks. When he gets to the mansion where he is staying, he finds a note from an 11-year-old boy asking him to take care of some pet fish.

SUNDAY
November 17

A great white albatross—the first in 100 years—is seen in California waters. It has a 7-foot wingspan.

WHO ELSE WAS BORN IN NOVEMBER?
VINCENT EDWARD ("BO") JACKSON

Football player and baseball player at Auburn University
In 1985, he won the Heisman Trophy, which is given annually to the nation's outstanding college football player.
BORN November 30, 1962, in Bessemer, Alabama

MONDAY
November 18

Enterprise, the space-shuttle prototype (original model), arrives in Washington, D.C., to become part of the Smithsonian Institution's National Air and Space Museum.

TUESDAY
November 19

President Reagan meets with Soviet leader Mikhail Gorbachev at the opening of the Geneva peace talks. Nancy Reagan has tea with Raisa Gorbachev.

WEDNESDAY
November 20

Rocket experiments by NASA cause the dawn sky from North Carolina to New York to turn weird shades of green and red.

THURSDAY
November 21

Hurricane Kate sweeps through Florida and Georgia, causing $1,000,000,000 in damage. • In the Sitra Channel in Bahrain, Roger Cranswick catches a world-record-breaking 17-pound, 4-ounce slender barracuda.

FRIDAY
November 22

In Seattle, Washington, 6 inches of snow has fallen, a record for the area. The temperature is 10°F, the second-coldest Seattle temperature in history.

SATURDAY
November 23

An unknown poem that may have been written by William Shakespeare is found in a library at England's Oxford University by a scholar from Topeka, Kansas.

SUNDAY
November 24

Pittsburgh, Pennsylvania, has been chosen America's number-one city by Rand McNally's *Places Rated Almanac*. Today thousands celebrate with performances and speeches.

MONDAY
November 25

The Statue of Liberty gets her new torch put on today. The 4,800-pound copper torch has been crafted from the statue's original design.

TUESDAY
November 26

Baseball's Yogi Berra gets 35,000 pounds of North Dakota potatoes dumped in his yard after he joked that North Dakota didn't "produce enough potatoes to fill my front lawn."

WEDNESDAY
November 27

Full Moon

A TON OF TURKEYS? "Daddy" Bruce Randolph prepares to serve 100,000 Thanksgiving dinners tomorrow at his Bar-B-Q restaurant in Denver, Colorado. The meals will be free!

THURSDAY
November 28

Thanksgiving. The crew of space shuttle *Atlantis* celebrates with a special dinner of rehydrated chicken consommé, smoked turkey irradiated with gamma rays, and thermostabilized cranberry sauce.

THE ERUPTION OF 1985

On November 13, Nevado del Ruiz, a volcano near Armero, Colombia, erupts in one of the worst volcanic disasters in history. A liquid avalanche of dirty water, gray ash, and mud cascades down its slopes, burying the sleeping town below. A Caribbean Airlines cargo plane accidentally flies into the erupting ash, which coats the pilot's windshield. Finally, he sticks his head out of the window in order to see where he can land!

FRIDAY
November 29

Two shuttle astronauts practice in-space construction techniques outside *Atlantis*, using what look like giant Tinkertoys, in order to see what it will be like to build stations in space.

SATURDAY
November 30

Salley, South Carolina, holds its 20th annual Chitlin Strut, featuring a parade, concerts, a hog-calling contest, and 25,000 pounds of hog intestines!

PRINCESS DIANA AND PRINCE CHARLES VISIT AMERICA TOGETHER FOR THE FIRST TIME

NATIONAL GUARD DROPS HAY FROM HELICOPTERS TO FEED STARVING CATTLE NEAR NEW ORLEANS

NEVADO DEL RUIZ, A VOLCANO DORMANT FOR 400 YEARS, EXPLODES VIOLENTLY IN COLOMBIA

December

December used to be the tenth month of the year (the Latin *decem* means "ten"). The old Roman calendar began with March.

BIRTHSTONE *Turquoise*

SUNDAY *December 1*	A zebra escapes from Hollywood Farms in Poolesville, Maryland.
MONDAY *December 2*	An early freeze on the upper Mississippi River traps more than 100 barges in ice. They may be stuck all winter.
TUESDAY *December 3*	The space shuttle *Atlantis* returns safely to Edwards Air Force Base in California. • Record low temperature in International Falls, Minnesota: −27°F
WEDNESDAY *December 4*	The U.S. Postal Service issues a 36-cent aerogramme to commemorate the 150th anniversary of both Mark Twain's birth and the appearance of Halley's comet, in 1835.
THURSDAY *December 5*	A 198-year-old bottle of wine, a 1787 Château Lafitte, is sold in London for $157,500. It was originally bottled for Thomas Jefferson. • Public television broadcasts a "children's summit"—between children in Moscow and children in Minneapolis, Minnesota.
FRIDAY *December 6*	A singing Christmas tree, 27-feet-tall and with 100 singing "ornaments," begins its performances in Charlotte, North Carolina.
SATURDAY *December 7*	The Heisman Trophy, recognizing the outstanding college football player of 1985, goes to Bo Jackson of Auburn University in Alabama. • Deer hunters in Maryland spot a zebra trotting along a road!
SUNDAY *December 8*	First day of Hanukkah • Ice-cold air from the North Pole enters the United States.
MONDAY *December 9*	Many schools in Wyoming and Colorado are closed because of 2 feet of snow and high winds. • In Dickerson, Maryland, coal-yard workers at a generating plant are startled when they see a zebra munching on grass nearby.

WHO ELSE WAS BORN IN DECEMBER?
LUDWIG VAN BEETHOVEN

German composer
Recognized as one of the greatest musical geniuses who ever lived, he composed many of his finest works while totally deaf.
BORN December 16, 1770, in Bonn, Germany

TUESDAY
December 10

FLYING SEA TURTLES: Four sea turtles in Atlantic City, New Jersey, that for some reason haven't migrated south, have been flown to Florida by airplane!

WEDNESDAY
December 11

The Statue of Liberty's face-lift is finished. The last of 7 spikes has been placed in her crown, and workers begin removing the scaffolding.

THURSDAY
December 12

WARBLER ALARM: In Denver, Colorado, Jane Axtell calls the Rare-Bird Alert Network after seeing a rare Cape May warbler pecking at a feeder in her yard.

FRIDAY
December 13

Friday the 13th, a day some people believe to be unlucky, occurs at least once every year but never more than 3 times in one year. There are 2 Friday the 13ths in 1985.

SATURDAY
December 14

A real gingerbread house is built at the American Festival Cafe in Rockefeller Center in New York City.

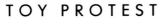

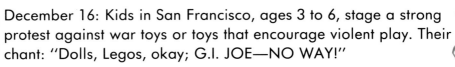

TOY PROTEST

December 16: Kids in San Francisco, ages 3 to 6, stage a strong protest against war toys or toys that encourage violent play. Their chant: "Dolls, Legos, okay; G.I. JOE—NO WAY!"

SUNDAY
December 15

Two wing-flap sections come off a jet on its way to Boston from London. The pieces fall from the sky and hit a house and a car in Revere, Massachusetts.

MONDAY
December 16

HAPPY BIRTHDAY, *PIONEER* 6! NASA sends radio signals to its oldest working satellite, 170,000,000 miles from earth. *Pioneer 6*, which was launched 20 years ago on this date, was expected to last only 6 months!

TUESDAY
December 17

A topaz gem as big as a cantaloupe, called the Brazilian Princess, has been donated anonymously to the American Museum of Natural History in New York City. It is 21,327 carats and is believed to be the largest cut stone in the world.

WEDNESDAY
December 18

The Disney Company and the French government agree on a Disneyland park to be built in France. It will be the first Disneyland in Europe and is expected to have 10,000,000 visitors a year.

TOY BOX '85

America's Top Playthings

The Pound Puppy
The Bubble Mower
Real Baby
My Buddy
G.I. Joe
Furskin
The World Travelers

My Li'l Stinker
She-Ra, Princess of Power
Wuzzle
Insectoids
Golden Girl
Teddy Ruxpin
Opus

Cabbage Patch Corner

The Cabbage Patch Kid
The Preemie
The Cabbage Patch Twins

THURSDAY
December 19

The launch of the space shuttle *Columbia* is postponed—14 seconds before liftoff—when a problem is found in the booster-rocket steering system.

FRIDAY
December 20

Former FBI clerk Randy Miles Jeffries is arrested on espionage charges. It is the 11th such arrest this year! Some people are calling 1985 the "Year of the Spy."

SATURDAY
December 21

Winter solstice • A sinkhole the size of a pickup truck is discovered in Keystone Heights, Florida, and it soon swallows a house and a carport! (Sinkholes are created when underground caverns lose water pressure that supports their roofs.)

SUNDAY
December 22

The space shuttle *Challenger* is hauled to the launching pad at Kennedy Space Center in Cape Canaveral, Florida, to get it ready for its January mission.

MONDAY
December 23

In Port Angeles, Washington, seabirds are cleaned, blow-dried, and fed by rescue workers after the birds were coated with oil in one of the worst oil spills in the state's history.

FUN FACT '85

The inventor of the earmuff was Chester Greenwood. Every year on December 21, his hometown of Farmington, Massachusetts celebrates Chester Greenwood Day!

Way to go Chester!

TUESDAY
December 24

Christmas Eve • A man in Kenosha, Wisconsin, is dropping 100-dollar bills in Salvation Army kettles if the bell ringer can say "Merry Christmas" in a foreign language. • It's a record 13th day of fog in Bakersfield, California.

WEDNESDAY
December 25

Christmas • Mount Etna erupts in Sicily with 4 rivers of red lava. • In Washington, D.C., the White House dinner includes President Reagan's favorite sweet treat: monkey bread.

THURSDAY
December 26

The World Enduro Championship Kart Races begin at Daytona International Speedway in Daytona Beach, Florida.

FRIDAY
December 27

Full Moon

Bird-watchers flock from hundreds of miles away to see a rare Cape May warbler, a bird usually found in South America that has moved into a backyard in Denver, Colorado.

SATURDAY
December 28

POUND PUPPY COUNT: Since they were introduced in April, 2,500,000 Pound Puppies have been sold. Each one comes with a cardboard doghouse and a Puppy Care sheet.

SUNDAY
December 29

A telethon called "Lou Rawls's Parade of Stars" ends today after raising $1,500,000 for the United Negro College Fund.

MONDAY
December 30

Mild earthquake in central Alaska. • The U.S. Bureau of the Census reports that as of July 1, 1985, the U.S. population was 238,740,000. California has the most people: 26,365,000.

TUESDAY
December 31

New Year's Eve • The deepest lake in the United States, Crater Lake in Oregon, is completely covered with ice for the first time in 37 years. • A special satellite hookup between the U.S. and the USSR allows people from the two countries to wish each other a happy New Year!

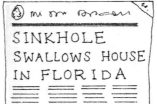

BIRDS COVERED WITH OIL FROM SPILL ARE WASHED AND BLOW-DRIED IN WASHINGTON STATE

SINKHOLE SWALLOWS HOUSE IN FLORIDA

DISNEY SIGNS AGREEMENT WITH FRANCE FOR FIRST DISNEY PARK IN EUROPE

YOUR YEAR AT A GLANCE

A lot happened the year you were born. How many events shown on the cover can you identify? Turn the page upside down for the answers.

1. Oldest person ever to climb Mount Everest reaches the top (April 30)   2. Soviet newspapers report a UFO sighting (January 30)   3. Georgia man begins 32-day stay in a pine tree (April 2)   4. International conference of scientists meet on the Ross Ice Shelf (January 9)   5. Dinosaur hunter sets out for the Congo (April 3)   6. The Titanic is found (September 1)   7. Japan agrees to end commercial whaling (April 5)   8. Top prize awarded in the All-American Turkey-calling Championship (April 6)   9. World's largest sand castle built in Treasure Island, Florida (April 28)   10. Dentist ordered to remove 4-foot-high tooth (November 15)   11. Black widow spiders turn up in car parts (July 18)   12. Zoo monkeys attempt clever escape (See August)   13. Texan first to see eclipse of Pluto (February 17)   14. International Tuba Day (May 5)   15. Student stuntman goes over Niagara Falls in a pickle barrel (August 18)   16. Poem possibly penned by William Shakespeare found (November 23)

973.9   Martinet, Jeanne
MAR   (Jeanne M.)

           1985, the year you
           were born.

$13.93

DATE			
9			

ANDERSON ELEMENTARY SCHOOL
5727 LUDINGTON
HOUSTON TX   77035

BAKER & TAYLOR BOOKS